THE **CAST-IRON SKILLET** COOKBOOK

THE CAST-IRON SKILLET COOKBOOK

Classic dishes and inspirational ideas for simple home cooking

RYLAND PETERS & SMALL
LONDON • NEW YORK

Designer Paul Stradling
Editor Kate Eddison
Production Controller Sarah Kulasek-Boyd
Art Director Leslie Harrington
Editorial Director Julia Charles
Publisher Cindy Richards

Indexer Hilary Bird

First published in 2015 by
Ryland Peters & Small
20–21 Jockey's Fields
London WC1R 4BW
and
341 E 116th St
New York NY 10029

www.rylandpeters.com

Text © Valerie Aikman-Smith, Maxine Clark,
Linda Collister, Felipe Fuentes Cruz and Ben
Fordham, Carol Hilker, Jenny Linford, Dan
May, Hannah Miles, Annie Rigg, Laura
Washburn and Ryland Peters & Small 2015

Design and photographs
© Ryland Peters & Small 2015

ISBN: 978-1-84975-662-4

10 9 8 7 6 5 4 3 2 1

A CIP record for this book is available from
the British Library.

US Library of Congress Cataloging-in-
Publication data has been applied for.

Printed and bound in China

NOTES

• Both American (Imperial plus US cups) and British (Metric) measurements are included in these recipes for your convenience; however it is important to work with one set of measurements and not alternate between the two within a recipe.

• All spoon measurements are level unless otherwise specified.

• All herbs are fresh unless otherwise specified.

• All fruit and vegetables should be washed thoroughly before consumption. Unwaxed citrus fruits should be used whenever possible.

• All eggs are large (US) or medium (UK), unless specified as US extra-large, in which case UK large should be used. Uncooked or partially cooked eggs should not be served to the very old, frail, young children, pregnant women or those with compromised immune systems.

• Ovens should be preheated to the specified temperatures. We recommend using an oven thermometer. If using a fan-assisted oven, adjust temperatures according to the manufacturer's instructions.

PICTURE CREDITS

Steve Baxter
Page 21

Peter Cassidy
Pages 5 (all except below left), 15,
22–26, 41, 42, 56

Richard Jung
Page 50

Erin Kunkel
Pages 11, 45

Steve Painter
Pages 1, 2, 5 below left, 8, 12, 19, 29,
33, 34, 37, 49, 52–53, 55, 59, 60, 63,
endpapers

William Reavell
Page 30

Kate Whitaker
Page 16

Isobel Wield
Pages 38–39

Polly Wreford
Page 46

CONTENTS

INTRODUCTION

Pots and pans are an essential feature of any kitchen, and none attracts such admiration as a cherished cast-iron skillet. We all have a variety of pans in diverse shapes and sizes hiding at the back of cupboards, which are designed for specific culinary purposes. However, the cast-iron skillet is so versatile, you may never need to use another pan again.

Cast-iron cookware is durable, relatively inexpensive and can last a lifetime. In fact, many people today use the same skillet their mother or grandmother used! Also there are many misconceptions about the difficulty in maintaining cast-iron pans, but follow a few simple rules, and you can use your skillet for years and years.

Cast iron distributes heat evenly, which makes it an excellent choice for cooking a wide variety of foods. When cleaned and seasoned properly, it has a non-stick surface that can rival any other non-stick coating, with the added bonus that it contains no chemicals. Seasoning the pan (see page 9) is simply coating the surface in oil and baking it at a high temperature until a natural non-stick coating is formed. The more you season the pan, the better the coating will be, and the more you use your pan, the more non-stick it will become.

WHAT YOU CAN COOK IN YOUR CAST-IRON SKILLET

A cast-iron skillet is extremely versatile and you can cook a wide variety of recipes in it. This single pan can be used for searing, stir-frying, sautéing, baking, or roasting. It gives the best results for cornbread, fried chicken, and blackened fish, and can be used to roast vegetables, fry pancakes, and even bake cakes. You can also use it to whip up a quick pizza at home—the hot cast-iron skillet acts just like a pizza stone to give you a crisp pizza base in next to no time. And why not use it instead of a pie dish? Simply cook the pie filling in the skillet, allow it to cool, then place your pastry lid over the top, crimp the edges, and cook in the oven. In fact, whatever your family favorite is, you can most likely cook it in a cast-iron skillet.

You can use it on the stovetop/hob, in the oven, on the outdoor grill/barbecue, or even over the campfire! Remember that the pan retains heat very well and the handle will get extremely hot and stay hot for a long time—always use thick oven mitts/gloves when handling your skillet, even when you think it may have cooled down.

If the pan is seasoned and maintained well, you can use your skillet to cook without any oil, making it one of the most old-fashioned methods of fat-free cooking. You may need to add a little oil to the pan for some delicate things, such as fried eggs, but once your seasoning is built up, you will find you need very little oil for other foods.

THINGS TO AVOID

Avoid cooking acidic foods, such as tomato sauces, in a cast-iron pan, as the acid can damage the seasoning. Never marinate food in your cast-iron skillet, and do not store food in the pan once it's cooked, especially anything that might be slightly acidic. Transfer the food to a suitable container, then clean and dry your skillet thoroughly, re-seasoning it if necessary.

Never pour cold water or other liquids onto the skillet while it is still hot, as it can cause the cast-iron to crack. Always allow your skillet to cool down before washing it.

Although a bit of soap won't hurt your cast-iron skillet when rinsed and dried well, it's best to avoid strong soaps. Don't use harsh scouring pads on the surface either, as you'll destroy all the seasoning you've built up. Avoid letting your skillet stay wet or having any prolonged contact with water. Dry it thoroughly (see page 9) and store it without the lid on to avoid any moisture building up.

ENAMELED CAST-IRON SKILLETS

You can also buy cast-iron skillets with a porcelain enamel coating, which have the durability and versatility of traditional seasoned cast-iron, but with the ease of not having to maintain the surface. Available in different colors, these pans have no exposed cast iron, so they can be used to cook acidic foods and are also suitable for storing and marinating food. Although many of these pans are designed to withstand the dishwasher, it's still always advisable to wash them by hand and dry them well to keep them in the best possible condition.

DOs AND DON'Ts

DO preheat your skillet before frying in it

DO lift your skillet rather than sliding it on to the stovetop/hob

DO use thick oven mitts/gloves when handling your skillet

DO wash your skillet after use with a little mild soap and water

DO dry your skillet thoroughly

DO season your skillet regularly

DO use the right size stove burner/hob ring for the pan

DON'T soak your skillet in water

DON'T put your skillet in the dishwasher

DON'T use any strong detergents or scouring pads

DON'T use your skillet in the microwave

DON'T leave your skillet with any trace of water on it

DON'T store your skillet with a lid on

DON'T marinate food in your skillet

DON'T store food in your skillet

DON'T put cold liquid into a hot pan

TAKING CARE OF YOUR SKILLET

Cast-iron skillets need a little love and care to be kept in the best possible condition. However, despite the myths about how difficult it is to maintain, cast iron is extremely durable, which is why people pass skillets down through their families for generations.

Cast iron is an alloy of molded iron, carbon, and silicon. It is a tough and rigid substance that will darken with use. It needs to be seasoned before you use it for cooking. Some cast-iron skillets are sold ready-seasoned, although these can still benefit from seasoning again at home before their first use. Enamel-coated cast iron does not need to be seasoned.

HOW TO SEASON YOUR CAST-IRON SKILLET

Cast-iron cooking utensils need to be seasoned before use to prevent rust from forming and food from sticking. It's an easy but effective process:

1. Preheat the oven to 300°F (150°C) Gas 3.

2. Wash the skillet in warm, soapy water, rinse thoroughly, and dry well.

3. Use a cloth or paper towel to coat the inside and outside surface of the skillet with a layer of vegetable oil.

4. Place the skillet upside-down in the centre of the preheated oven. Bake for 1 hour.

5. Turn off the heat and allow the skillet to cool in the oven before removing.

HOW TO CLEAN YOUR CAST-IRON SKILLET

You need to clean your skillet after each use—don't be scared of washing it, there are just a few simple rules to follow. Never soak cast-iron, as it can cause the pan to rust. It's a good idea to clean it quite soon after use, rather than letting the food get stuck onto the pan. However, do let the pan cool completely before washing it, as running cold water into a hot skillet can cause it to crack. When the skillet is cool enough to handle, follow this simple step-by-step procedure:

1. Wash the skillet in warm, soapy water, scrubbing it gently to remove any bits of stuck-on food from the bottom.

2. Rinse the skillet with clean water to remove any excess soap.

3. Place the wet skillet on the stovetop/hob over a high heat to dry, then add a little vegetable oil and rub it all over the pan using a cloth or paper towel.

4. Leave the pan over the heat until it is just starting to smoke, then carefully rub it once more with oil.

5. Turn off the heat and let cool.

KIMCHI HASH BROWNS WITH POACHED EGGS

1 large Russet/Maris Piper potato, washed and shredded

2 garlic cloves, finely minced

salt and pepper

3 tablespoons olive oil, plus extra to serve

4 eggs

1 tablespoon vinegar

a bunch each of flat leaf parsley and Thai basil (or regular basil), torn

SPICY KIMCHI

½ small Napa/Chinese cabbage, halved

½ small Savoy cabbage, halved and core removed

⅓ cup/75 g sea salt

1 large carrot, shredded

2 scallions/spring onions, thinly sliced

1-inch/2.5-cm piece of fresh root ginger, peeled and shredded

2 radishes, shredded

1 Persian cucumber, shredded

¼ cup/60 ml rice wine vinegar

1 tablespoon fish sauce

1 tablespoon chile/chilli paste

SERVES 4

If you are having friends over for Sunday brunch, try these glorious hash browns, served with a Bloody Mary. The kimchi must be made at least a week in advance, but you could always use store-bought kimchi instead.

Make the kimchi a week in advance. Slice the cabbages into 1-inch/2.5-cm strips and put in a large ceramic bowl. Dissolve the salt in 3 cups/700 ml water and pour over the cabbage. Cover with plastic wrap/clingfilm and let stand at room temperature for 8–24 hours. Drain the cabbage and place back in the bowl with the carrot, scallions/spring onions, ginger, radishes, and cucumber. Add the vinegar, fish sauce, chile/chilli paste, and ½ cup/120 ml water, and mix. Spoon into sterilized jars and pour over any remaining juice. Screw the lids on and leave at room temperature for 24 hours. Refrigerate for at least 5 days (or up to 6 weeks) before serving.

Mix together the grated potato, garlic, and kimchi in a large mixing bowl. Season with salt and pepper. Heat a large cast-iron skillet over medium–high heat and add the olive oil. When the oil starts to sizzle, add the potato–kimchi mix and brown for 2 minutes. Reduce the heat and continue to cook, stirring occasionally, for another 6–8 minutes. You want the hash browns to be crispy and browned.

Crack the eggs into separate small bowls. Fill a medium skillet three-quarters of the way up with water. Add the vinegar and place over medium heat until bubbles start to form in the bottom. Carefully pour the eggs one at a time into the water, making sure they are spaced apart. Cook for 4 minutes, then remove with a slotted spoon, gently shaking off any excess water. Place on top of the hash browns, and sprinkle with the torn parsley and Thai basil leaves.

Finish with a drizzle of olive oil and a sprinkle of salt and pepper.

MAINE LOBSTER OMELET

According to food lore, the omelet/omelette has been around since the 16th century, so what better pan to use for this classic dish than your cast-iron skillet? Since then, many variations have emerged, from the ham, green (bell) pepper, and onion combination from Denver to *khagineh*, an Iranian version in which eggs are beaten with sugar. This lobster dish is popular on the East Coast of the US, and is especially decadent with the truffle-Hollandaise sauce.

6 eggs

6 oz./170 g fresh cooked lobster meat, chopped

2 teaspoons unsalted butter

sea salt and ground black pepper

4 oz./115 g tomatoes, chopped

1 teaspoon snipped/chopped chives

TRUFFLE-HOLLANDAISE SAUCE

3 egg yolks

¼ cup/60 ml water

2 tablespoons freshly squeezed lemon juice

1 stick/115 g unsalted butter, chilled and cut into pieces

¼ teaspoon sea salt

a pinch of ground black pepper

a pinch of paprika

a drizzle of truffle oil

1 chive, snipped/chopped, to garnish

a 10-inch/25-cm cast-iron skillet

SERVES 2

Preheat an oven to 210°F (100°C) Gas ¼.

To make the truffle-Hollandaise sauce, beat the egg yolks, water, and lemon juice in a small saucepan until blended. Cook over very low heat, stirring continuously, until the mixture bubbles at the edges. Stir in the butter, a piece at a time, until it has melted and until the sauce has thickened. Remove from the heat immediately and stir in the salt, pepper, paprika, and truffle oil. Transfer the sauce to a small pot and garnish with the snipped/chopped chive, ready to serve.

Beat the eggs together, then divide the mixture among two bowls and set aside.

Spread the lobster onto an oven-proof dish and place in the preheated oven for 5 minutes.

Over medium heat, warm the cast-iron skillet and, when hot, add 1 teaspoon of the butter and swirl the pan to make sure the surface is coated. As the butter melts, season one portion of the eggs with salt and black pepper. Add this egg mixture to the heated skillet and stir very gently with a spatula.

As the eggs start to set, add half of the warmed lobster, half of the tomatoes, and half of the chives to the eggs and stir gently. As the eggs start to set, stop stirring and let them firm for 1–2 minutes. Fold the omelet/omelette and slide it out onto a warm plate. Place the plate in the oven to keep the omelet/omelette warm. Repeat the same process for the second omelet/omelette, making sure the skillet is greased with the remaining butter before you add the eggs.

SCRAMBLED EGGS WITH CHORIZO

Just as they are all over the world, eggs are a very popular way to start the day in Mexico. They are usually scrambled (*huevos revueltos*) and mixed with a variety of ingredients. This simple skillet recipe uses chorizo and the key is to make sure that you don't scrimp on its quality. Mexican chorizo usually comes as ground meat, but this recipe uses the Spanish sausage found in most supermarkets and it works very well. Most chorizo is a deep reddish color and the color seeps out into the eggs to give them a lovely orange tint. There is also a fantastic green chorizo in Mexico that is made with a combination of tomatillos, chile/chilli peppers, and garlic—it is worth trying it if you ever get the chance.

4 eggs

1 teaspoon olive oil

3½ oz./100 g chorizo, finely sliced

¼ onion, finely chopped

½ cup/50 g shredded Monterey Jack or Cheddar cheese

SERVING SUGGESTION
flour tortillas, warmed

refried black or pinto beans

salsa of your choice

SERVES 2

Break the eggs into a medium mixing bowl and beat well with a fork.

Set a cast-iron skillet over medium heat and, when it is hot, add the oil—you only need a very small amount because the chorizo will release some of its own oils on cooking.

Add the chorizo and fry for about 20 seconds, then add the onion and fry for another 20 seconds, stirring continuously.

Add the eggs and scramble, stirring to break up the eggs, for 1–2 minutes.

Remove from the heat, transfer to a serving dish, and sprinkle the cheese over the top.

Serve with warm tortillas, refried beans, and your favorite salsa, if you like.

SPICY BACON CORNBREAD

The bacon gives a wonderful flavor to this recipe. Dry-cured, smoked, fatty/streaky bacon works very well, but everyone has a particular favorite type of bacon to use. The same goes for the chile/chilli; put in just what you like and what will work best with other dishes. This cornbread is excellent eaten with a thick lentil or pea soup. A skillet is perfect for this recipe, because you can bake the bread in it after you've used it to cook the bacon.

6 slices/rashers bacon, finely chopped

2 scallions/spring onions, chopped

1 medium–hot chile/chilli pepper, or to taste, chopped

1 cup/130 g unbleached all-purpose/plain flour

1 cup/150 g yellow cornmeal, preferably stone-ground

½ teaspoon baking soda/bicarbonate of soda

1 teaspoon baking powder

¼ teaspoon sea salt

1 cup/250 ml buttermilk

1 tablespoon clear honey

1 US extra-large/UK large egg

3 tablespoons/40 g butter, melted

a 9-inch/23-cm cast-iron skillet

MAKES 1 MEDIUM BREAD (SERVES 6–8)

Preheat the oven to 400°F (200°C) Gas 6.

Put the chopped bacon in a cold skillet and cook gently over low heat until the fat begins to run and the bacon becomes golden and crisp. Stir in the chopped scallions/spring onions and the chile/chilli, then remove the pan from the heat and set aside to cool.

In a large mixing bowl, combine the flour, cornmeal, baking soda/bicarbonate of soda, baking powder, and salt.

In another bowl, beat together the buttermilk, honey, egg, and melted butter. Add this mixture to the dry ingredients and mix thoroughly with a wooden spoon. Stir in the cooled bacon, scallions/spring onions, and chile/chilli from the skillet.

Scrape the mixture into the greasy skillet and spread evenly.

Bake for 20 minutes in the preheated oven until firm to the touch. Best eaten warm the same day. Can be frozen for up to 1 month—reheat thoroughly before serving.

PANCAKES WITH WHIPPED MAPLE BUTTER

The classic American-style pancake is light and fluffy. A cast-iron skillet holds heat very well, so it is ideal for making pancakes. You will need to grease it with butter before making each pancake, and check the pan is hot enough before you add the batter. Serve these straight away rather than storing them in the refrigerator, otherwise the butter will set and lose its fluffy texture. Alternatively, serve these pancakes with crispy bacon and maple syrup instead.

1¼ cups/160 g self-rising/self-raising flour, sifted

1 teaspoon baking powder

1 egg, separated

1 teaspoon pure vanilla extract

scant ⅓ cup/60 g granulated/caster sugar

a pinch of sea salt

1 cup/250 ml milk

3 tablespoons/40 g butter, melted, plus extra for frying

MAPLE BUTTER

1 stick/115 g butter

¼ cup/60 ml maple syrup, plus extra to serve

½ cup/60 g confectioners'/icing sugar, sifted

MAKES 12

To make the pancake batter, put the flour, baking powder, egg yolk, vanilla extract, granulated/caster sugar, salt, and milk in a large mixing bowl and beat together. Add in the melted butter and beat again. The batter should have a smooth, dropping consistency.

In a separate bowl, whip the egg white to stiff peaks. Gently fold the whipped egg white into the batter mixture using a spatula. Cover and let rest in the refrigerator for 30 minutes.

For the maple butter, whip together the butter, maple syrup, and confectioners'/icing sugar using an electric beater until light and creamy. This is best made shortly before serving.

When you are ready to serve, remove your batter mixture from the refrigerator and stir once. Set a large cast-iron skillet over medium heat and heat up. Add a little butter and let melt and coat the bottom of the skillet, then ladle small amounts of the rested batter into the pan, leaving a little space between each, or if you want to make larger pancakes, fill the pan to make one at a time. Cook until the underside of each pancake is golden brown and a few bubbles start to appear on the top—this will take about 2–3 minutes. Turn the pancakes over using a spatula and cook on the other side until golden brown. Cook the remaining batter in the same way, in batches, until it is all used up, adding a little butter to the pan each time to prevent sticking.

Serve the pancakes in a stack with a little maple butter and a drizzle of maple syrup on top.

LIGHT DISHES

CHORIZO & OLIVES IN RED WINE
WITH PADRÓN PEPPERS

This dish makes a lovely appetizer or nibble selection for a drinks party. Padrón peppers are small, strongly flavored green peppers that are pan-fried, seasoned with sea salt, and eaten whole. Look for them in Spanish delis. If you can't get hold of them, use green (bell) peppers, seeded and sliced, instead.

5 oz./150 g chorizo

1 garlic clove, peeled and bruised

1 sprig of fresh thyme

⅔ cup/150 ml red wine

1 tablespoon sherry vinegar or balsamic vinegar

2 tablespoons mixed olives in olive oil, plus 1 tablespoon oil from the jar

1 tablespoon chopped flat leaf parsley

5 oz./150 g Padrón peppers

sea salt flakes

SERVES 4

Cut the chorizo into bite-size chunks. Heat a cast-iron skillet over medium heat, add the chorizo, and cook until it starts to brown and crisp at the edges. Add the bruised garlic, leaves from the thyme sprig, and red wine to the pan and continue to cook over medium heat until the red wine has reduced by half. Add the vinegar and cook for 30 seconds or so. Add the olives and chopped parsley.

Meanwhile, heat the tablespoon of olive oil from the jar of olives in another skillet and add the whole Padrón peppers. Cook over medium heat until hot and starting to brown at the edges. Season with salt flakes and serve with the chorizo.

MINI CRAB CAKES WITH QUICK CHILE LIME MAYO

Nothing represents all that is wonderful and surprising about seafood better than the humble crab. Hidden behind a most unlikely exterior, its flavorful, succulent, and incredibly versatile meat is a delight. Fresh crab combines wonderfully well with chile/chilli. These mini crab cakes, served with the quickest chile lime mayo, are great as nibbles with a glass of white wine.

1 lb. 2 oz./500 g lump/cooked white crabmeat

4 scallions/spring onions, finely chopped

1 garlic clove, crushed

1 hot red or green chile/chilli pepper, seeded and very finely chopped

1 tablespoon chopped fresh flat leaf parsley or cilantro/coriander

1 tablespoon nam pla, or other fish sauce

1 teaspoon raw cane/muscovado or soft light brown sugar

1 egg, beaten

1 teaspoon white wine vinegar

a good pinch of sea salt

all-purpose/plain flour, to dust

½ cup/100 ml sunflower or peanut/groundnut oil, for frying

QUICK CHILE LIME MAYO

4 tablespoons mayonnaise

finely grated zest and juice of 1 lime

1 red chile/chilli pepper, finely chopped

MAKES 16

Mix together the crabmeat, scallions/spring onions, garlic, chile/chilli, herbs, fish sauce, sugar, egg, vinegar, and salt. This can most easily be done in a food processor; however, mixing by hand in a bowl will give more texture to the final crab cakes.

Divide into 16 pieces and shape into balls, then flatten into discs. Dust each crab cake lightly with flour and refrigerate for 30 minutes before cooking. This makes them easier to handle and less likely to fall apart during cooking.

Meanwhile, mix together the quick chile lime mayo ingredients.

Heat the oil in a large cast-iron skillet over medium heat and, once hot, fry the crab cakes in small batches. Turn frequently and when both sides are golden—about 2 minutes each side—they are ready to serve.

Serve with the quick chile lime mayo for dipping.

FRIED GREEN TOMATOES

Fried green tomatoes are especially popular in the Southern States of the US, and they are perfect for cooking in your skillet. This recipe is simple to prepare—frying unripened tomatoes in vegetable oil after coating them with a mixture of flour, cornmeal, and a little salt and pepper. Panko bread crumbs are ideal and are available from large supermarkets or Asian food stores.

4 large green tomatoes

2 eggs

½ cup/125 ml milk

1 cup/120 g all-purpose/plain flour

½ cup/65 g cornmeal

½ cup/60 g panko or ordinary dry bread crumbs

2 teaspoons coarse sea salt

¼ teaspoon ground black pepper

vegetable oil, for frying

SERVES 4

Chop the tomatoes into ½-inch/1.25-cm slices, discarding the ends. You should have 4–5 pieces per tomato. Set aside.

In a medium mixing bowl, whisk the eggs and milk together.

Measure out the flour and put it on a plate. In a separate bowl, beat together the cornmeal, bread crumbs, salt, and pepper, then transfer the mixture to a plate.

First, dip the tomato slices into the flour to coat, then dip them into the milk and egg mixture. Finally, dip them into the bread crumb mixture so that they are completely coated.

Pour vegetable oil to a depth of ½ inch/1.25 cm into a large cast-iron skillet and heat over medium heat. When the oil is steadily bubbling, carefully place the tomatoes into the skillet in batches of 4 or 5, depending on the size of your skillet. Do not crowd the tomatoes—they should not touch each other. When the tomatoes are browned, flip and fry them on the other side. Drain them on paper towels.

BUFFALO WINGS WITH HOMEMADE
RANCH DRESSING

1 cup/140 g all-purpose/plain flour

½ teaspoon paprika

½ teaspoon cayenne pepper

½ teaspoon sea salt

20 chicken wings

vegetable oil, for frying

celery and carrots, for dipping

RANCH DRESSING

1 cup/250 ml buttermilk, shaken

¼ cup/60 g mayonnaise

3 tablespoons sour cream

3 tablespoons finely chopped fresh flat leaf parsley

2 tablespoons finely chopped fresh chives

4 teaspoons white wine vinegar or freshly squeezed lemon juice

1 garlic clove, finely chopped

¼ teaspoon garlic powder

½ teaspoon sea salt, plus extra if needed

2 pinches of ground black pepper, plus extra if needed

HOT SAUCE

1 stick/115 g butter

½ cup/125 ml Louisiana hot sauce, or other hot pepper sauce

2 pinches of ground black pepper

3 pinches of garlic powder

MAKES 20

Taking their name from the city in which they originated (Buffalo, New York), Buffalo wings have become an American staple. They are often served during sporting events or at late-night bars, but are great to serve at home.

Combine the flour, paprika, cayenne pepper, and salt in a large resealable plastic bag. Shake the bag to combine the spices. Next, put the chicken wings in the bag, seal tightly, and shake them to coat evenly in the spice mix. Place the bag in the refrigerator for 60–90 minutes.

Place all of the ranch dressing ingredients in a 2-cup/500-ml jar with a tight-fitting lid. Seal tightly and shake to evenly distribute all the ingredients. Taste and season with additional salt and pepper as desired. Refrigerate until chilled and the flavors have melded, about 1 hour. The dressing will last up to 3 days in the refrigerator.

For the hot sauce, combine the butter, Louisiana or other hot pepper sauce, ground black pepper, and garlic powder in a small saucepan over low heat. Warm until the butter is melted and the ingredients are well blended. Set aside.

In a large, deep, cast-iron skillet, add the vegetable oil to a depth of 1–2 inch/2.5–5 cm and heat to 375°F (190°C) or until the oil is bubbling steadily. Put the wings into the heated oil and fry them for 10–15 minutes, or until some parts of the wings begin to turn a golden to dark brown color and they are cooked through.

Remove the wings from the oil and drain on paper towels for a few seconds. Place the wings in a large bowl or in a large uncovered Tupperware box. Add the hot sauce mixture and stir, tossing the wings to thoroughly coat them.

Serve with the homemade ranch dressing and with a few sticks of celery and carrot for dipping.

SPANISH TORTILLA WITH ROASTED
PIQUILLO PEPPERS

Here are simple ingredients, carefully cooked with a little chile/chilli twist. It really is hard to go wrong with a tortilla. Eaten hot or cold, this makes a lovely appetizer, lunch, or light meal. It is worth remembering that this is nothing like a French omelet/omelette; it requires comparably long and gentle cooking. Like the Italian frittata, it is, however, always worth the wait.

3 tablespoons olive oil

2 large white onions, thinly sliced

2 large potatoes, peeled and thinly sliced

sea salt and ground black pepper

4 roasted Piquillo peppers (available in jars in olive oil), drained and roughly chopped

6 eggs

green salad, to serve (optional)

an 8-inch/20-cm cast-iron skillet

SERVES 6 AS AN APPETIZER OR 4 AS A LIGHT MEAL

Heat half of the oil in the cast-iron skillet, add the onions and potatoes, and toss to coat. Season well and add the Piquillo peppers. Turn down the heat and cover with a lid. Cook until the potatoes and onions are soft and translucent, about 20 minutes. Turn regularly to prevent too much browning. Once they are softened, remove them from the oil with a slotted spoon and set aside.

Lightly beat the eggs in a large mixing bowl and add the onions and potatoes (they should still be hot so that the cooking process of the eggs begins as soon as they are mixed together). Season with salt and pepper. Add the rest of the oil to the skillet and return to medium heat. Pour the egg mixture into the hot pan—it should fill it by about two-thirds. Turn the heat down to its lowest setting and cook for 20–25 minutes until there is very little liquid on the surface.

Preheat a broiler/grill and place the skillet under the broiler/grill to cook the tortilla for another 2–3 minutes. Serve with a green salad, if you like.

BUTTERNUT SQUASH & CHILE TATIN

As an alternative to the popular French sweet dessert tatins, this is a savory version, packed with butternut squash and warming chile/chilli. It is delicious served warm accompanied by Greek-style yogurt and a dressed green salad.

1 large butternut squash

⅓ cup/80 ml olive oil

5 sprigs of fresh thyme

2 garlic cloves, sliced

2 whole large red chile/chilli peppers

sea salt and ground black pepper

GLAZE

2 tablespoons/30 g butter

1 tablespoon granulated/caster sugar

1 tablespoon balsamic vinegar

PASTRY

1¼ cups/150 g all-purpose/plain flour, sifted, plus extra for dusting

6 tablespoons vegetable shortening, chilled and shredded OR 1¼ cups/90 g shredded beef or vegetable suet

sea salt and ground black pepper

about ½ cup/120 ml milk

an 8-inch/20-cm cast-iron skillet, greased

SERVES 4–6

Preheat the oven to 350°F (180°C) Gas 4.

Cut the squash in half and remove the seeds using a spoon, then cut it into 1-inch/2.5-cm slices, leaving the skin on if you wish. Put the squash in a roasting pan and drizzle with the olive oil. Add the thyme, garlic, and chiles/chillies to the pan, season with salt and pepper, and roast for about 40 minutes until the squash is soft but still holds its shape and is starting to caramelize. Remove from the oven and let cool slightly. If you are going to be cooking the tart immediately, leave the oven on.

For the glaze, heat together the butter, sugar, and vinegar in a small saucepan until thin and syrupy, then pour it into the skillet. Scatter the roasted chiles/chillies and thyme sprigs on the bottom of the skillet and arrange the roasted butternut squash slices in a pattern on top.

To make the pastry, mix together the flour and vegetable shortening/suet, and season with salt and pepper. Add the milk gradually (you may not need it all depending on the absorption rate of your flour, which differs from brand to brand) and bring the mixture together into a soft dough.

Preheat the oven again to 350°F (180°C) Gas 4.

On a flour-dusted surface, roll out the dough to a circle just larger than the size of the skillet. Using a rolling pin, gently lift the pastry circle on top of the butternut squash in the pan and press it down tightly. Patch any cracks with pastry trimmings. Bake the tatin in the preheated oven for 20–25 minutes until the pastry is golden brown. Remove from the oven, invert onto a serving plate, and serve straight away.

AVOCADO, REFRIED BEAN & MONTEREY JACK SANDWICH

This sandwich is great any time of day, either as is or with a fried egg on top. For extra heat, use spicy refried beans. Any kind of salsa will go with this, but tomatillo salsa has a bit more tang to offset the richness of the cheese.

unsalted butter, softened

4 slices white bread

scant 1 cup/200 g refried beans

1 ripe avocado, pitted/stoned, peeled and sliced

1⅓ cups/150 g shredded Monterey Jack or mild Cheddar cheese

TOMATILLO SALSA

3 tomatillos or tomatoes, finely chopped

1 small red (bell) pepper, seeded and roughly chopped

2 scallions/spring onions, finely chopped

1 green chile/chilli pepper, finely chopped

a bunch of fresh cilantro/coriander, finely chopped

a pinch of sea salt

SERVES 2

Butter the bread slices on one side and arrange buttered-side down on a clean work surface or cutting board. Spread the beans on the non-buttered side.

Put two slices of bread in a cast-iron skillet, butter-side down. If you can only fit one slice in your skillet, you'll need to cook one sandwich at a time. Arrange half of the avocado slices on top of each slice of bread, then sprinkle over half of the cheese in an even layer. Cover with another bread slice, butter-side up.

Turn the heat to medium and cook the first side for 3–5 minutes until deep golden, pressing gently with a spatula. Carefully turn with a large spatula and cook on the second side, for 2–3 minutes more, or until deep golden brown all over.

Meanwhile, make the salsa by combining all the ingredients and mixing thoroughly.

Remove the sandwiches from the skillet, transfer to a plate, and cut in half. Let them cool for a few minutes before serving with the salsa.

CHIPOTLE CHICKEN, GREEN BELL PEPPER & QUESO FRESCO SANDWICH

If poblano peppers are available, use them here instead of the green (bell) peppers for a more authentic touch of Southwestern spice.

2 tablespoons vegetable oil

1 chipotle chile/chilli in adobo sauce, plus 1 teaspoon sauce, finely chopped

freshly squeezed juice of 1 lime

2 boneless skinless chicken breasts (about 10 oz/300 g)

a pinch of sea salt

1 green (bell) pepper, cored and thinly sliced

unsalted butter, softened

1 round brown loaf, cut in half widthwise and lengthwise to form 4 triangular slices

2 thin slices mild cheese, such as Gouda or Fontina

¾ cup/100 g crumbled queso fresco or feta

a small handful of fresh cilantro/coriander, finely chopped

SERVES 2

Preheat the oven to 350°F (180°C) Gas 4.

In a small bowl, combine 1 tablespoon of the vegetable oil with the chile/chilli and lime juice, and mix well. Coat the chicken breasts with this mixture and season with the salt. Transfer to a baking pan and bake in the preheated oven until cooked through, 20–25 minutes. Let cool, then slice thinly.

Meanwhile, combine the remaining oil and (bell) pepper strips in a small cast-iron skillet and cook until softened and lightly charred. Set aside.

Butter all the bread slices on one side and set aside.

Unless, you have a really large skillet, you'll need to cook these sandwiches one at a time. Put one slice of bread in a cast-iron skillet, butter-side down. Put one slice of cheese on top, then spread half of the chicken slices on top of the cheese. Arrange half the pepper strips on top and sprinkle with half of the crumbled cheese and cilantro/coriander. Cover with another bread slice, butter-side up.

Turn the heat to medium and cook the first side for 4–5 minutes until deep golden, pressing gently with a spatula. Carefully turn with a large spatula and cook on the second side, for 2–3 minutes more, or until deep golden brown all over.

Remove from the skillet, transfer to a plate, and let cool for a few minutes before serving. Repeat for the remaining sandwich.

HAM & APPLE SKILLET PIE

1 lb./450 g cooked ham, diced

3 tablespoons all-purpose/plain flour, seasoned with sea salt and ground black pepper

2 tablespoons soft light brown sugar

¼ teaspoon freshly grated nutmeg

¼ teaspoon ground allspice

1 lb./450 g cooking apples, peeled, cored, and quartered

2 onions, thinly sliced

1¼ cups/300 ml dry (hard) cider

sea salt and ground black pepper

SUET CRUST PASTRY

1¾ cups/225 g all-purpose/plain flour, plus extra for dusting

½ teaspoon fine sea salt

2½ tablespoons/50 g lard, chilled and cut into pieces

⅔ cup/50 g shredded beef or vegetable suet

1 teaspoon dried mixed herbs

2–3 tablespoons ice-cold water

3–4 tablespoons milk, to glaze

a 10-inch/25-cm cast-iron skillet

SERVES 4–6

Serve this with a robust vegetable such as broccoli, cabbage, or sprouts and boiled, buttered new potatoes.

Preheat the oven to 400°F (200°C) Gas 6.

To make the pastry, sift the flour and salt into a large mixing bowl, add the lard, and rub in with your fingertips until combined. Stir in the suet and herbs, and mix to a soft dough with just enough of the water to bind. Knead lightly until smooth, then cover and leave to rest in a cool place until required.

Toss the diced ham in the seasoned flour to coat lightly. Mix the sugar and spices together in a separate bowl.

Put half of the ham in the cast-iron skillet and cover with half of the apples, then half of the spice mixture and half of the onion slices. Repeat these layers, seasoning between each one, then pour in the cider.

On a lightly floured surface, roll out the pastry to a circle the diameter of the skillet and make a small slit in the center. Place the pastry over the skillet and press it around the edge of the skillet. Crimp the edge of the pastry. Brush the pastry with milk, place the skillet in the preheated oven, and bake for 20 minutes. Reduce the temperature to 350°F (180°C) Gas 4 and bake for another hour until golden (covering the top with kitchen foil if you feel the pastry is becoming too dark).

GROUND BEEF TACOS

This is one of the best-loved taco fillings, and it's great for whipping up in a skillet. A well-seasoned ground beef filling is always a winner.

2 tablespoons vegetable oil

1 small onion, grated

2 generous teaspoons ground cumin

½ teaspoon dried hot pepper flakes/chilli flakes

1 tablespoon dried oregano

2 garlic cloves, crushed

1 green chile/chilli pepper, very finely chopped

1 lb 2 oz./500 g ground beef/beef mince

1 teaspoon fine sea salt

freshly squeezed juice of ½ lime

a small handful of chopped fresh cilantro/coriander

6–12 flour tortillas, warmed

TO SERVE

shredded Cheddar or Monterey Jack cheese

crisp lettuce, thinly sliced

tomato salsa

SERVES 4–6

Heat the oil in a cast-iron skillet set over medium–high heat. Add the onion, cumin, dried hot pepper flakes/chilli flakes, and oregano and cook for 1–2 minutes, stirring often, until aromatic.

Add the garlic and fresh chile/chilli and cook for 1 minute. Add the beef and salt, and mix to combine and break up the beef. Cook for 8–10 minutes, stirring occasionally, until well browned.

Taste and adjust the seasoning. Add the lime juice and cilantro/coriander and stir well.

To serve, put a generous helping of beef in the middle of each tortilla. Top with shredded cheese, lettuce, and spoonfuls of salsa. Serve immediately with extra salsa on the side.

DINER CHEESEBURGER

According to food historians, the cheeseburger was invented in 1920 in Pasadena, California, a remarkable 20 years after the hamburger first appeared. Lionel Sternberger (no pun intended), a cook at his father's sandwich shop "The Rite Spot", one day decided to place a slab of American cheese on a hamburger, inventing one of the world's most loved sandwiches.

1 lb./450 g ground beef/ beef mince

1 cup/140 g minced onion

2 garlic cloves, crushed

sea salt and ground black pepper

olive oil, for frying

8 slices/rashers fatty/streaky bacon

4 eggs

4 brioche buns, sliced in half

4 slices American or Cheddar cheese

1 dill pickle, thinly sliced

ranch dressing, to serve (optional)

dill pickle relish, to serve (optional)

DIJONNAISE
2 large white onions

¼ stick/25 g butter

1⅔ cups/400 ml light/single cream

3 tablespoons Dijon mustard

a pinch each of sea salt, ground black pepper, garlic powder, freshly grated nutmeg, chopped fresh flat leaf parsley and chopped fresh tarragon

MAKES 4

First, make the Dijonnaise by finely chopping the white onions and frying in the butter in a medium skillet. Add the cream and mix in the mustard. Add the various seasonings and simmer until the sauce takes on a mustardy color and is relatively thick.

Mix together the beef, minced onion, and garlic. Shape into patties and sprinkle with salt and pepper. Heat a cast-iron skillet over medium heat and add 1 tablespoon oil. Add the patties and cook for about 4 minutes on each side, or until cooked to your liking. Remove from the skillet and keep warm.

Add the bacon to the skillet and cook until crisp. Remove the bacon from the skillet and keep warm. Add some more oil to the skillet, if needed, and fry the eggs until cooked to your liking.

Spread a layer of Dijonnaise on each brioche bun, place a cooked patty on top, then a slice of cheese, followed by a fried egg, 2 slices/ rashers of bacon, and some dill pickle slices.

Serve with ranch dressing and some dill pickle relish, if you like.

STEAK SANDWICH WITH SAUTÉED ONIONS & BLUE CHEESE

A good steak sandwich isn't always the easiest to come by. It's hard to find the right combination of perfectly spiced steak, topped with a bounty of trimmings that add the right amount of flavor and texture when placed on a crispy loaf of bread. This sandwich with rare steak, sautéed onions, Dijonnaise, arugula/rocket, and blue cheese on French country bread is the answer!

2 x 12 oz./350 g New York strip/sirloin steaks, cut 1 inch/2.5 cm thick

sea salt and ground black pepper

olive oil, for frying

4 onions, sliced into rings

½ teaspoon fresh thyme leaves

2 garlic cloves, minced

1–2 loaves French country bread

4 tablespoons Dijonnaise (page 40)

1 cup/30 g arugula/rocket

4–8 oz./115–225 g blue cheese, crumbled

potato wedges or fries, to serve

MAKES 4

Season the steaks with salt and pepper on both sides. Heat 2–4 tablespoons olive oil in a cast-iron skillet over high heat until it's very hot, almost smoking. Sear the steaks for 1½ minutes per side and then reduce the heat to low and cook for 3–4 minutes, turning once. Remove the steaks from the skillet and place on a plate. Cover tightly with kitchen foil and let sit in the refrigerator for 10 minutes. Remove and slice the steak into strips.

Using the same skillet, heat 3 tablespoons more olive oil over medium heat. Add the onion slices and thyme and sauté for about 10 minutes, stirring occasionally, until the onion is caramelized. Add the garlic for the last 1–2 minutes.

Cut the French country bread lengthwise into large sandwich rolls. Spread 1 tablespoon Dijonnaise on the bottom half of each bun. Place a layer of the steak strips on top of the Dijonnaise, sprinkle with salt and pepper, and top with the caramelized onion rings. Place the arugula/rocket on top of the onion rings and sprinkle a handful of blue cheese on top. Cover with the top halves of the buns and serve with potato wedges or fries.

HOGWILD BOURBON PORK CHOPS
WITH APPLES

This is definitely a dish for bourbon lovers. The pork chops are marinated overnight in a hogwild bourbon glaze, then cooked in a smoking-hot cast-iron skillet with apples. This dish soaks up everything great about the Southern States of America: pork, bourbon, honey, and molasses/black treacle.

4 center-cut pork chops, bone in

2 Granny Smith apples, cored and sliced into wedges

HOGWILD BOURBON GLAZE

½ cup/120 ml bourbon

2 tablespoons molasses/black treacle

1 tablespoon clear honey

½ teaspoon chipotle chili/chilli powder

2 garlic cloves, roughly chopped

2 tablespoons chunky orange marmalade

2 tablespoons olive oil

1 sprig of fresh rosemary

sea salt and ground black pepper

SERVES 4

To make the hogwild bourbon glaze, put all the ingredients in a blender or food processor and process until puréed and smooth. The glaze may be stored in an airtight container in the refrigerator for up to 2 weeks.

Rinse the pork chops in cold water and pat dry with a paper towel. Put the chops in a ceramic baking dish and pour over the hogwild bourbon glaze (save some to pour over the cooking pork and apples; see below). Cover and put in the refrigerator for 8–24 hours to let the marinade flavors soak in.

After this time, remove the marinated pork from the refrigerator and let it come to room temperature.

Heat a large cast-iron skillet over medium–high heat until just smoking. Remove the chops from the marinade, place in the hot skillet, and reduce the heat to medium. Brown the chops for 3–5 minutes per side.

Meanwhile, pour the remaining glaze into a separate pan and bring to a boil. Reduce the heat and simmer the glaze until reduced by half.

Once the chops have browned, add the apple slices to the skillet with the pork and turn down the heat. Pour over the reduced glaze and cover. Cook for another 5 minutes, or until cooked to your liking.

Cook's Note: Due to the high alcohol and sugar content of the glaze, if you are cooking over gas the glaze may ignite into a small flame. Don't be alarmed; just let the alcohol burn off and the flame will die out—it only takes a few minutes.

BUTTERMILK FRIED CHICKEN

Making a marinade with buttermilk to coat drumsticks before frying them makes for tender, flavorful chicken. This is a thoroughly tasty dish, and very much a family favorite. Serve with crunchy slaw on the side.

2 garlic cloves, crushed

1 thumb-size piece of fresh ginger, crushed

½ teaspoon chili/chilli powder

1 teaspoon chopped fresh thyme leaves

1¼ cups/300 ml buttermilk

sea salt and ground black pepper

8 chicken drumsticks

1½ cups/200 g all-purpose/plain flour

1 teaspoon ground ginger

sunflower oil, for deep-frying

slaw, to serve

SERVES 4

In a large mixing bowl, mix together the garlic, ginger, chili/chilli powder, thyme, and buttermilk to make the marinade. Season well with salt and ground black pepper.

Add the chicken drumsticks to the marinade bowl and coat them well. Cover and marinate in the refrigerator for 8 hours, or overnight.

In a separate bowl, mix together the flour and ground ginger, and season with salt and pepper. Transfer this flour mixture to a large plate.

Shake any excess marinade from the chicken drumsticks and coat them thoroughly in the seasoned flour.

Pour the oil into a large, deep cast-iron skillet to around ¾ inch/2 cm in depth and let the pan become very hot. Test that the pan is the right heat by dropping in a small piece of bread; if it turns brown very quickly, the oil is hot enough.

Add in the chicken drumsticks (cooking them in batches if the pan isn't large enough for them all) and fry until they are a rich golden brown on all sides and cooked through, around 15–20 minutes. Remove the chicken drumsticks from the skillet, let them rest on paper towels or another absorbent surface to soak up the oil, then serve immediately with some slaw.

CAJUN-STYLE BLACKENED FISH
WITH MAQUE CHOUX

4 fresh catfish fillets, or other thin skinless fish fillets

1 stick/115 g butter, melted

CAJUN SPICE SEASONING

1 teaspoon ground black pepper

1 teaspoon celery seeds ground in a pestle and mortar with 1 teaspoon sea salt flakes

½–1 teaspoon cayenne pepper

2 tablespoons smoked sweet paprika (Spanish pimentón dulce)

1 tablespoon garlic powder

1 tablespoon dried oregano

1 tablespoon dried thyme

MAQUE CHOUX

¼ stick/25 g butter

1 cup/115 g finely chopped onion

½ red (bell) pepper, seeded and chopped

2 cups/280 g fresh corn/sweetcorn kernels

¾ cup/180 ml heavy/double cream

1 teaspoon chopped fresh thyme

½ teaspoon Tabasco sauce or similar, or to taste

1 scallion/spring onion, chopped

2 tablespoons chopped fresh flat leaf parsley

1 tablespoon chopped fresh basil

sea salt and ground black pepper

SERVES 4

Blackening fish in a cast-iron skillet creates juicy, perfectly cooked fillets in a matter of minutes and the crust of spices and herbs is packed with flavor yet light to eat. The ideal accompaniment here is maque choux, a traditional Cajun dish from southern Louisiana.

To make the maque choux, melt the butter in a large cast-iron skillet over medium–high heat. Add the onion and sauté for 5 minutes until translucent. Add the red (bell) pepper and cook for about 3 minutes until softened. Add the corn and cook for 2 minutes. Add the cream, thyme, and ½ teaspoon of Tabasco. Simmer for about 5 minutes until the sauce thickens. Stir in the scallion/spring onion, parsley, and basil. Season to taste with salt, pepper, and more Tabasco, if liked. Cover the pan with kitchen foil or a plate and set aside until ready to serve. The maque choux should be served warm.

When you are ready to cook the fish, place your skillet over the hottest burner you have and heat for 3–4 minutes, until very hot indeed (open a window if you can!). Meanwhile, prepare the Cajun spice seasoning by simply mixing all the ingredients together and then tip it into a shallow dish large enough to take a fish fillet. Pour the melted butter into a shallow dish of similar proportions and set it next to the one with the spice mix.

First dip the fish fillets into the melted butter and then press each one into the spice mix to thoroughly coat on both sides.

When the skillet is smoking hot, lay the fish fillets in it—as many as you can fit in comfortably without overcrowding the pan. Cook for about 2–3 minutes on each side (using a metal spatula to turn them over) until the spices are blackened and burned onto the fillets to form a crust, and the flesh is opaque and flakes easily.

Serve immediately with the maque choux on the side.

GARLIC MUSHROOM SKILLET PIZZA

Make super-fast, super-easy pizzas at home in a cast-iron skillet. Cast-iron retains heat very well, so you will achieve a perfect crispy base without having to heat a pizza stone first. You can add whatever toppings you like, but this garlic mushroom topping is delicious.

1 cup/50 g fresh bread crumbs

¼ cup/30 g freshly grated Parmesan cheese

4 garlic cloves, finely chopped

4 tablespoons chopped fresh parsley

¼ stick/25 g butter, melted

about 12 medium cremini/chestnut mushrooms

2–3 oz./50–75 g buffalo mozzarella or cow's milk mozzarella, excess water drained and cut into cubes

extra virgin olive oil, to drizzle

sea salt and ground black pepper

PIZZA DOUGH

½ cake/12 g compressed/fresh yeast, ½ tablespoon dried active yeast, or 1 teaspoon fast-action dried yeast

¼ teaspoon sugar

½ cup/125 ml hand-hot water

2 cups/250 g '00' flour, plus extra for dusting

½ teaspoon fine sea salt

2 tablespoons olive oil, plus extra for oiling

a 10-inch/25-cm cast-iron skillet

MAKES 1 PIZZA

First make the pizza dough. In a medium mixing bowl, cream the compressed/fresh yeast with the sugar and beat in the hand-hot water. Leave for 10 minutes until frothy. For other yeast, follow the manufacturer's instructions. Sift the flour and salt into a large bowl and make a well in the center. Pour in the yeast mixture, then the olive oil. Bring the dough together with your hands, then tip out onto a floured surface and knead for 5–10 minutes until smooth and elastic. Place into an oiled bowl, cover with plastic wrap/clingfilm, and let rise for about 1 hour 30 minutes, or until doubled in size.

Preheat the oven to 425°F (220°C) Gas 7 for at least 30 minutes.

Mix the bread crumbs with the Parmesan, garlic, and parsley, then stir in the melted butter. Lightly fill the cavities of the mushrooms with the bread crumb mixture.

Place the cast-iron skillet over medium heat until it is very hot.

Uncover the dough, punch out the air, and roll or pull into a 10-inch/25-cm circle. Carefully place the dough in the hot cast-iron skillet. Arrange the mozzarella over the pizza crust leaving a 1-inch/2.5-cm rim around the edge. Arrange the stuffed mushrooms all over, sprinkling any remaining bread crumbs over the finished pizza. Drizzle with extra virgin olive oil and season. Cook on the stovetop/hob until the edge of the pizza is risen and starting to look cooked.

Place the skillet in the preheated oven and cook for about 30 minutes, or until the crust is golden, the cheese melted, and the mushrooms tender and bubbling. Remove from the oven and drizzle with extra virgin olive oil. Eat immediately.

MUSHROOM & TALEGGIO MAC 'N' CHEESE WITH TARRAGON

It is the addition of tarragon to this recipe that transforms it from an ordinary mushroom and cheese dish into something truly sublime. Be sure to use the fresh herb, as dried is simply not the same.

a handful of coarse sea salt

1 lb. 2 oz./500 g macaroni

10 oz./300 g portobello mushrooms, stems trimmed level with caps

2–3 tablespoons vegetable oil

fine sea salt and ground black pepper

leaves from a few sprigs of fresh parsley, finely chopped

leaves from a few sprigs of fresh tarragon, finely chopped

2½ cups/600 ml heavy/double cream

scant 1 cup/100 g shredded Cheddar cheese

½ cup/50 g shredded Parmesan cheese

8 oz./250 g Taleggio cheese, thinly sliced

a 10-inch/25-cm cast-iron skillet

SERVES 6–8

Add the coarse sea salt to a pan of boiling water and cook the macaroni according to the package instructions. When cooked, drain, rinse well under running water, and let dry in a colander.

Preheat the oven to 400°F (200°C) Gas 6.

Arrange the mushrooms in a single layer on a baking sheet, stems up, and brush with the oil. Season lightly with salt, sprinkle over the herbs, and roast for 15–20 minutes until tender. Remove and let cool slightly. Slice the mushrooms and set aside.

Preheat the broiler/grill to medium.

Put the cream in a large cast-iron skillet and bring just to a boil, stirring occasionally, then reduce the heat. Add the Cheddar and Parmesan and half of the Taleggio, and stir well to melt. Taste and adjust the seasoning. Remove from the heat.

Add the cooked macaroni and stir in half of the sliced mushrooms. Spread the mixture evenly in the skillet. Top with the remaining mushrooms and Taleggio slices and a good grinding of black pepper.

Broil/grill for 5–10 minutes until the top is golden, and serve immediately.

PEACH COBBLER

This is a classic American dessert and it works very well in a cast-iron skillet. It should be eaten soon after baking because the cobbler dough soaks up the fruit juices while standing, but that doesn't mean you should overlook it as a breakfast option the next day. Add a basket of blackberries to the peaches, if you like, or use a combination of peaches, apricots, and blackberries.

6 peaches, not too ripe

1 tablespoon all-purpose/plain flour

1 tablespoon freshly squeezed lemon juice

3 tablespoons clear honey

cream or vanilla ice cream, to serve

COBBLER TOPPING

½ cup/125 ml heavy/double cream

⅓ cup/75 ml sour cream or crème fraîche

1¾ cups/230 g all-purpose/plain flour

¼ cup/50 g granulated/caster sugar, plus extra for sprinkling

1 teaspoon baking powder

¼ teaspoon baking soda/bicarbonate of soda

a pinch of fine sea salt

½ stick/60 g unsalted butter

6 individual 6-inch/15-cm cast-iron skillets, well-buttered

MAKES 6

Preheat the oven to 375°F (190°C) Gas 5.

Cut the peaches in half, remove the pits/stones, then cut each half into 3 slices. Divide them among the individual skillets (or use one large skillet), sprinkle with the flour, and toss well to coat evenly. Add the lemon juice and honey and stir. Set aside.

To make the topping, put the cream and sour cream or crème fraîche in a mixing bowl and stir well. Set aside.

Put the flour, sugar, baking powder, baking soda/bicarbonate of soda, and salt in a large mixing bowl and mix well. Add the butter, in small pieces, and rub in with your fingertips until the mixture resembles coarse bread crumbs. Using a fork, stir in the cream mixture until blended—use your hands at the end if necessary; it should be sticky, thick, and not willing to blend easily.

Drop spoonfuls of the mixture on top of the peaches, leaving gaps to expose the fruit. Sprinkle sugar liberally on top of the batter. Bake in the preheated oven until golden, 25–35 minutes. Serve warm with cream or ice cream.

PLUM & HAZELNUT PANDOWDY

A pandowdy is usually made with a rolled sweet dough or dough baked on top of fruit, the crust being "dowdied" by pushing the sweet dough into the fruit juices to soften it before serving. It can also be served upside down like a French tarte tatin—the key thing is that the dough will soak up some of the wonderfully fruity juices.

2 lbs./900 g mixed plums

½ cup/100 g soft light brown sugar

½ teaspoon ground cinnamon

finely grated zest and juice of 1 small orange

3 tablespoons/40 g unsalted butter, chilled and cut into pieces

PANDOWDY CRUST

2 cups/260 g all-purpose/plain flour, plus extra for dusting

3 tablespoons superfine/caster sugar, plus extra for dusting

1 tablespoon baking powder

1 stick less 1 tablespoon/100 g unsalted butter, chilled and cut up

1 cup/70 g finely ground hazelnuts

about 1 cup/250 ml light/single cream, plus extra to serve

an 8-inch/20-cm cast-iron skillet

SERVES 6

Preheat the oven to 425°F (220°C) Gas 7.

Cut the plums in half, discard the pits/stones, and slice them thickly. Mix them with the brown sugar, cinnamon, and orange zest and juice in a bowl. Tip the fruit into the cast-iron skillet and dot with the butter.

To make the pandowdy crust, sift the flour, sugar, and baking powder into a large mixing bowl. Rub the chilled butter into the flour with your fingertips until the mixture resembles coarse bread crumbs. Add the ground hazelnuts and mix. Stir in all but a couple of tablespoons of the cream with a blunt knife until the dough comes together. It will be sticky. Knead very lightly until smooth.

Working quickly, roll out on a lightly floured surface to a circle ¼ inch/5 mm thick and ½ inch/1 cm wider than the skillet. With the help of the rolling pin, lift the dough over the fruit and over the edge of the skillet. Do not press the crust onto the sides of the pan. Make a couple of slits in the dough to let the steam escape. Brush with the remaining cream and dust with sugar.

Stand the skillet on a baking sheet to catch any leaking juices and bake in the preheated oven for 10 minutes, then reduce to 350°F (180°C) Gas 4 and loosely cover with kitchen foil. Bake for another 35–40 minutes, until the crust is golden.

Remove from the oven and "dowdy" the crust by sharply pushing it under the surface of the bubbling fruit with a large spoon. Serve warm with cream.

TARTE TATIN

Which apple variety to use for a tarte tatin is the source of much debate. Golden Delicious hold their shape well and have a mild flavor that complements the rich caramel, but some people prefer a sharper variety. The most important thing is to use one that holds up to cooking.

1¼ sticks/150 g unsalted butter

¾ cup/150 g granulated/caster sugar

3 lbs./1.5 kg (about 9) Golden Delicious or tart apples such as Granny Smith, peeled, cored, and quartered

sour cream or crème fraîche, to serve

PASTRY

1½ cups/200 g all-purpose/plain flour, plus extra for dusting

2 teaspoons superfine/caster sugar

1 stick less 1 tablespoon/100 g unsalted butter, chilled and cut into pieces

a pinch of fine sea salt

3–4 tablespoons cold water

an 8-inch/20-cm cast-iron skillet

SERVES 6

To make the pastry, put the flour, sugar, butter, and salt in a food processor and, using the pulse button, process the mixture until combined (about 5–10 pulses). Add 3 tablespoons cold water and pulse again until the dough forms crumbs or holds together; add 1 tablespoon more water if necessary. Form the dough into a ball, cover it, and let it rest for 30–60 minutes in a cool place.

On a floured work surface, roll out the pastry to a circle the diameter of the skillet; turn the skillet upside-down on the rolled-out dough and trace around it with the tip of a sharp knife. Transfer the pastry circle to a baking sheet and chill until needed.

Put the butter and sugar in the skillet and set over high heat. Melt, stirring continuously to blend. Remove from the heat and arrange the apple quarters in the pan in two circles. The inner circle should go in the opposite direction to the outer circle.

Return to the heat and cook for about 30 minutes. From this point, watch the apples carefully and cook for another 5–15 minutes until the liquid thickens and turns a golden caramel color.

Meanwhile preheat the oven to 400°F (200°C) Gas 6.

Remove the skillet from the heat and top with the pastry circle, carefully tucking in the edges. Transfer to the preheated oven and bake until browned, about 45–60 minutes. Remove from the oven and let cool only slightly. Unmold while still warm or the caramel will harden, making it too difficult. To do this, carefully invert the tart onto a serving plate so that the pastry is on the bottom. Serve hot, warm, or at room temperature with sour cream or crème fraîche.

APPLE BROWN BETTY WITH DRIED CRANBERRIES

This is another traditional American recipe with very humble origins. It is always made with apples, but not necessarily dried cranberries. Just like English bread pudding, it is an economic way to use up stale bread, but it tastes even better if you use fresh white bread or even brioche.

2 lbs./900 g tart apples, such as Granny Smith or Cox's Orange Pippin, peeled, cored, and diced

1 teaspoon ground cinnamon

1 tablespoon finely grated orange zest

⅓ cup/75 ml apple or orange juice

⅔ cup/100 g dried cranberries

7 cups/375 g fresh white bread crumbs

¾ stick/85 g unsalted butter, melted

⅔ cup/80 g chopped pecans

⅓ cup/75 g soft light brown sugar

¼ stick/30 g unsalted butter, chilled and cut into pieces

whipped cream, to serve

a 10-inch/25-cm cast-iron skillet, well-buttered

SERVES 4–6

Preheat the oven to 375°F (190°C) Gas 5.

In a bowl, combine the apples, cinnamon, orange zest, apple or orange juice, and cranberries. Toss gently with your hands to mix. Set aside.

In a separate bowl, combine the bread crumbs and melted butter and mix well.

Spread about one-third of the buttered bread crumbs in the bottom of the prepared skillet. Add the pecans and sugar to the remaining bread crumbs and mix to combine.

Put half of the apple mixture on top of the bread crumbs in the skillet. Top with half of the bread crumb and pecan mixture. Top this with the remaining apple mixture and finish with the remainder of the bread crumb and pecan mixture. Dot with the chilled butter and bake in the preheated oven until golden, about 30–40 minutes. Serve warm with whipped cream.

BLUEBERRY SKILLET CAKE WITH WHIPPED LEMON CREAM

2 eggs

1 stick/115 g unsalted butter, melted

1 cup/200 g granulated/caster sugar

1 teaspoon pure vanilla extract

1 cup/250 ml whole/full-fat milk

2 cups/260 g all-purpose/plain flour

1½ teaspoons baking powder

½ teaspoon baking soda/bicarbonate of soda

½ teaspoon fine sea salt

2 cups/250 g fresh blueberries (or 10-oz/285-g package of frozen if not in season)

WHIPPED LEMON CREAM

1 cup/250 ml whipping cream

3 tablespoons confectioners'/icing sugar, sifted, plus extra for dusting

3 teaspoons freshly squeezed lemon juice

2 teaspoons finely grated lemon zest

a 10-inch/25-cm cast-iron skillet, well buttered

SERVES 8

This is a deliciously moist cake with a soft crumb. Packed with juicy fresh blueberries, a slice served with whipped lemon cream is the perfect fork cake for coffee time or an indulgent dessert that makes the most of the summer glut of blueberries.

To make the lemon cream, beat the cream with an electric beater on high speed until it begins to thicken. Gradually beat in the sugar. Continue beating and add the lemon juice a little at a time. Beat until soft peaks form. Fold the lemon zest in by hand. Spoon into a serving bowl, cover with plastic wrap/clingfilm, and refrigerate until needed.

Preheat the oven with the cast-iron skillet inside to 350°F (180°C) Gas 4.

In a large mixing bowl, lightly beat the eggs, then add the melted butter, sugar, vanilla extract, and milk and beat to combine.

Sift the flour, baking powder, and baking soda/bicarbonate of soda into a separate mixing bowl and add the salt. Pour in the egg mixture and mix by hand until just combined. Fold in the blueberries.

Carefully remove the hot skillet from the oven. Pour or spoon the batter into the hot skillet and use a metal spatula/palette knife to level the top.

Return the skillet to the preheated oven and bake the cake for about 30 minutes until a knife or metal skewer inserted in the center comes out clean.

Once the cake is cooked, dust lightly with confectioners'/icing sugar and serve warm or at room temperature with a few spoonfuls of the chilled whipped lemon cream on the side.

INDEX

RECIPE CREDITS

Valerie Aikman-Smith
Kimchi Hash Browns with Poached
 Eggs
Hogwild Bourbon Pork Chops with
 Apples

**Ben Fordham and Felipe Fuentes
Cruz**
Scrambled Eggs with Chorizo

Maxine Clark
Garlic Mushroom Skillet Pizza
Ham & Apple Skillet Pie
Plum & Hazelnut Pandowdy

Linda Collister
Spicy Bacon Cornbread

Carol Hilker
Maine Lobster Omelet
Fried Green Tomatoes
Buffalo Wings with Homemade
 Ranch Dressing
Diner Cheeseburger
Steak Sandwich with Sautéed Onions
 & Blue Cheese

Jenny Linford
Buttermilk Fried Chicken

Dan May
Mini Crab Cakes with Quick Chile
 Lime Mayo
Spanish Tortilla with Roasted Piquillo
 Peppers

Hannah Miles
Pancakes with Whipped Maple Butter
Butternut Squash and Chile Tatin

Annie Rigg
Chorizo & Olives in Red Wine with
 Padrón Peppers

Laura Washburn
Avocado, Refried Bean & Monterey
 Jack Sandwich
Chipotle Chicken, Roasted Green
 Bell Pepper & Queso Fresco
 Sandwich
Mushroom & Taleggio Mac 'N'
 Cheese with Tarragon
Ground Beef Tacos
Tarte Tatin
Apple Brown Betty with Dried
 Cranberries
Peach Cobbler

Ryland Peters & Small
Cajun-style Blackened Fish with
 Maque Choux
Blueberry Skillet Cake with Whipped
 Lemon Cream